Resolving Conflict Successfully

Needed Knowledge and Skills

Neil H. Katz
John W. Lawyer

CORWIN PRESS, INC.
A Sage Publications Company
Thousand Oaks, California

For information address:

Corwin Press, Inc.
A Sage Publications Company
2455 Teller Road
Thousand Oaks, California 91320

SAGE Publications Ltd.
6 Bonhill Street
London EC2A 4PU
United Kingdom

SAGE Publications India Pvt. Ltd.
M-32 Market
Greater Kailash I
New Delhi 110 048 India

Printed in the United States of America

Library of Congress Cataloging-in-Publication Data

Katz, Neil H.
    Resolving conflict successfully : needed knowledge and skills /
Neil H. Katz, John W. Lawyer.
        p.   cm. — (Roadmaps to success)
    Includes bibliographical references.
    ISBN 0–8039–6145–6 (pbk.)
    1. School management and organization—United States. 2. School
administrators—United States. 3. Conflict management—United
States. 4. Educational leadership—United States.   I. Lawyer, John
W. II. Title. III. Series.
LB2806.K278   1994
371.2'01—dc20   93–44469

94 95 96 97 98   10 9 8 7 6 5 4 3 2 1

Corwin Press Production Editor: Marie Louise Penchoen

Contents

Foreword

Neil Katz and John Lawyer continue their series of very enlightening books in this new book, *Resolving Conflict Successfully: Needed Knowledge and Skills*. This is the second in a three-book series dealing with research findings and exemplary practices related to the issue of conflict resolution. The first volume, published in 1993, is entitled *Conflict Resolution: Building Bridges*. It introduces a useful model for dealing with conflict, delineating four stages for conflict resolution: awareness, self-preparation, conflict management, and negotiation. The third volume, soon to be published, will further amplify the insights on conflict resolution they have already presented.

This second volume discusses the critical skills of communication, building rapport, listening, pacing, chunking, and problem solving. It provides a generic problem-solving model to assist the practitioner in applying the principles of their Conflict Resoluton Model to most negotiation situations.

A series of 20 figures help illustrate the concepts discussed in the text, and an application from Katz and Lawyer's own experience provides a real-life illustration of principles at work. Finally, an annotated bibliography directs the reader to additional in-depth knowledge of the conflict-resolution topic.

This book is an invaluable aid to all those in education who deal with conflict-resolving and problem-solving situations during their work days. It is a MUST READ for all who wish to understand the art of negotiation and who wish to resolve conflicts in an efficient, effective, and compassionate manner.

JERRY J. HERMAN
JANICE L. HERMAN
Series Co-Editors

About the Authors

Neil H. Katz is committed to self-actualization, nonviolence, and participative decision making as a way to influence change among individuals and in organizations and society. His primary interest is facilitating interactive learning and skill development about conflict and its resolution.

Katz serves in a leadership capacity in five different conflict resolution programs in the Maxwell School of Citizenship and Public Affairs at Syracuse University. He is the Director of the Program in Nonviolent Conflict and Change, Director of the Annual Summer Institute on Creative Conflict Resolution, Director of the University Conflict Resolution Consulting Group, Faculty Supervisor of the Campus Mediation Center, and Associate Director of the Program on the Analysis and Resolution of Conflicts.

Katz is a Danforth Teaching Fellow, a process consultant, a mediator, a facilitator, and a trainer in conflict resolution and negotiation skills. His clients include organizations in education, ministry, government, and education. Among his educational clients are the Danforth Foundation, the New York State Council of Superintendents, the New Jersey Department of Education, the U.S. National Science Foundation, the St. Louis Principal's Association, and numerous school systems in New York State and around the country.

Before receiving his doctorate and becoming a college professor, he taught junior high school.

Katz is the author or coauthor of over 20 book chapters and articles on conflict resolution and nonviolence and coauthor (with Jack Lawyer) of three highly acclaimed workbooks, *Communication Skills for Ministry, Communication and Conflict Resolution Skills,* and *Communication and Conflict Management Skills.*

John W. Lawyer enjoys difference and change. He values himself as a choice maker and creator of processes and models that enable people to become lifelong learners. His primary interest is enabling others to build trusting environments, learn from their experience, and develop increasing autonomy in their professional and personal lives. In his work in facilitating change in organizations, Lawyer believes that creating dignity, meaning, and community in the workplace enables people to support and be committed to the idea behind their work. In this way work becomes satisfying, and both the organization as a whole and its members learn and develop.

In 1976 Lawyer founded Henneberry Hill Consultants, Inc., and currently serves as its president. It is an association of professional consultants dedicated to helping individuals, groups, and organizations improve their overall effectiveness in achieving their interests and goals. As a process consultant, he serves clients in education, business, government, social service, and church-related systems. Prior to entering the consulting business, Lawyer managed an international business in which he pioneered the principle that leadership's primary task is to build trust, promote learning from experience, and enable people and work teams to achieve autonomy. These concepts were introduced in three of seven foreign manufacturing plants and one major domestic manufacturing plant.

Lawyer has a special interest in the development of models and skills for conflict management and interest-based negotiation. He has, in collaboration with others, published five books in the field of conflict resolution and change. He has been teaching three courses in Syracuse University's Summer Sessions in the Institute on Creative Conflict Resolution since 1979.

Introduction

This book is the second of a three-volume work on conflict resolution for educational administrators. In the first volume, *Conflict Resolution: Building Bridges* (1993), we presented the nature and sources of conflict, the benefits of a positive attitude toward conflict, and a particular model and process to manage and resolve conflicts effectively and efficiently in the interdependent world of today's schools.

The Conflict Resolution Model delineated in our first book consists of four stages: awareness, self-preparation, conflict management, and negotiation. At the heart of the model are two distinct communication processes: conflict management and negotiation (see Figure I.1).

Conflict management is a communication process for changing destructive emotional states into constructive states that allow working out a joint solution into a conflict. *Negotiation* is a communication process for enabling disputing partners to achieve a mutually agreed-on outcome with respect to their differences. The particular approach to negotiation advanced in this model is interest-based negotiation leading to integrated agreements. The problem-solving process embedded in the negotiation strategy is used to

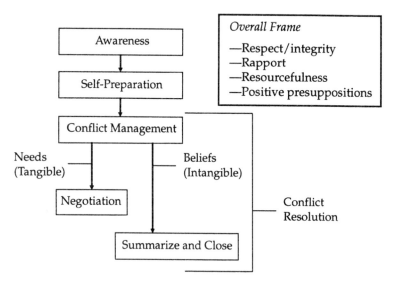

Figure I.1. Conflict Resolution—Working Model

allow the free creation of ideas that will best meet the needs of the disputing parties.

The success of the Conflict Resolution Model and its attendant processes of conflict management and negotiation relies heavily on some specific core knowledge and skills that are essential to achieving win/win outcomes. In this book, we focus on this critical knowledge —highly refined communication and rapport-building strategies—and the skills essential for achieving effective communication in a conflict context. Four core skills are introduced: reflective listening, laser listening, pacing, and chunking.

This knowledge and these skills are fundamental to resolving conflict successfully. As a guide to using these tools, we present in chapter 3 a generic problem-solving model as an essential ingredient in negotiation. And as an example of the Conflict Resolution Model in action, in chapter 4 we offer a real-life application from our own experience.

Communication and Rapport

In numerous studies of successful school administrators, it was found that the ability to communicate effectively ranks as a key characteristic. Administrators spend much of their workday speaking and listening as they provide leadership for school personnel. The ability to communicate accurately and efficiently and build trust and credibility with their communication partners is essential for effective leadership and conflict resolution. Knowing how to build rapport and communicate well enables those in conflict situations to convey their intention and meaning with appropriate precision.

Communication is the verbal or nonverbal exchange between parties during which each party influences the experience of the other. Anything you do to influence another's experience at both the conscious and unconscious levels is communication. Communication involves an exchange of thoughts and feelings to achieve meaning; the intention behind communication is to transfer meaning. Information is exchanged through words; voice tone, timbre, and tempo; and physiology. Physiology involves facial expression, body movement, body posture, and breathing patterns.

Rapport is a shared psychological state between people who are responsive and attentive to one another. The mutual state of rapport describes a state of trust between people.

Rapport and effective communication are essential for getting individual needs met, for developing significant interpersonal relationships, and for functioning well in society. Effective communicators have three abilities in common:

1. *Outcome:* Good communicators know their intended outcome. They are clear on the results they intend to accomplish by a particular communication and what those results would look, sound, or feel like. Part of this clarity results from having no conflicting desired outcomes.
2. *Flexibility:* Good communicators have adequate flexibility to vary their communication until they achieve their outcome. If what they are doing is not moving in the desired direction, they have the ability to change what they are doing until their outcome is achieved. They have different styles and techniques for approaching the same goal with different people at different times.
3. *Awareness:* Good communicators are aware of the responses to their communication. Being able to see and hear with precision are major competencies of effective communicators. They can notice subtle shifts in another's physiology and use these as signals for varying their method of presentation. They are responsive to the reactions of those receiving their communication.

In communicating with another, you choose a manner of expressing, or encoding, the information you wish to convey. The other then interprets, or decodes, your information and receives some impact from it. The goals for effective communication are mutual understanding and meaning. Your outcome is to ensure that the impact of your communication on another matches your intention and that the impact of another's message on you corresponds with the other's intention. The cyclic process is illustrated in Figure 1.1.

This communication process involves the use of specific skills. For instance, when conveying information, you can learn ways of expressing yourself effectively and testing to be sure that your in-

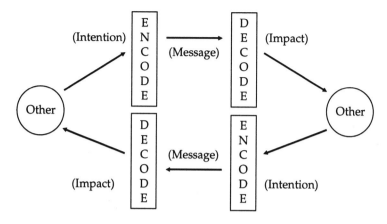

Figure 1.1. Communication Process

Based on Thomas Gordon, *Teacher Effectiveness Training* (New York: Peter H. Wyden, 1974) pp. 66-69.

formation is understood. When receiving information, you can learn ways of listening effectively to be sure you are understanding the other.

Communication involves filters. Any external event is filtered, including the sounds we hear, things we see, and spoken and written communications. These filters are unconscious. They are accumulated in our personal history through our life experience. We form perceptions based on this filtered information, but we generally are not consciously aware of how we are filtering our experience or how close our perceptions are to reality. For instance, if you have a friend who you think is intelligent, you have at least one "filter" operating whenever your friend does or says anything. You will tend to perceive your friend's behavior as intelligent. In contrast, if you're communicating with someone you dislike or that you believe is dishonest, but who says exactly the same thing, your perception will be different. The information reaches our brain changed in many ways from the original information.

In the communication process, these filters include our beliefs, personal style, past experiences, and even the way our brains operate. These filters play an enormous role in creating our perception of what someone said or meant in a communication. We always respond to our perception of what someone meant as if it

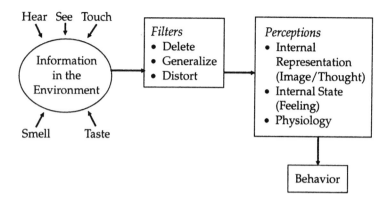

Figure 1.2. A Communication Model

were reality. Our perception of information drives our behavior, not the information itself. This process occurs on both sides of the conversation.

A communication model illustrating how filters operate is presented in Figure 1.2. Information reaches our brain through these filters. We generalize, distort, and delete information based on our personal history. Within the brain we experience a perception, usually in the form of an image and sounds. Almost instantly an internal state (a feeling) emerges and our physiology adjusts to reflect this image and internal state. Our behavior flows from this perception of reality.

An underlying principle for effective interpersonal communication is that the emotions must be dealt with before anything else. When a person is experiencing strong feelings, he or she cannot think clearly, respond logically, or solve problems effectively. This is true whether the emotions are positive or negative. Figure 1.3 illustrates "Emotional Normal" and a situation when strong negative feelings crowd out our ability to think rationally.

When emotions are strong, more primitive brain functioning is engaged, leaving little room for rational thinking or problem solving. The use of effective skills allows all participants in the communication to function at the highest level with an appropriate balance of thoughts and feelings. After emotions are heard, your best rational thinking can take place.

"Emotional Normal" has thoughts and feelings in balance:

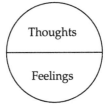

When, for whatever reason, a person's negative feelings become prominent, the imbalance looks like this:

anger
impatience
hurt
annoyance
indifference
distrust
pressured
cheated

Figure 1.3. Emotional Responses

The first step in becoming an effective communicator is to know what you want—your specific outcome. The second step is to uncover the outcome(s) of those with whom you are in communication. Successful communication happens when you can achieve your outcome and enable the other to achieve his or her outcome at the same time. This process is one of fitting together outcomes so that both parties in the communication experience understanding and meaning.

Communication involves speaking and listening at both verbal and nonverbal levels. It involves words and physiology, including body posture and voice tone, tempo, patterns, shifts, rhythms, repetitions, and variations. *Speaking* is expressing your thoughts and feelings with precision. Your intention is to convey information clearly and accurately through words and behavior so that the likelihood of the other understanding your meaning is increased. *Listening* is taking in information and forming a hypothesis about the meaning of what another is saying from his or her particular perspective. The ability to speak and listen effectively to achieve your communication outcomes requires sensory acuity, flexibility, congruence, and personal integrity.

- *Sensory acuity* is being curious about and noticing changes and responses in another during the communication process through your senses, especially seeing and hearing.
- *Flexibility* is being responsive to changes noticed in another's words and behavior and choosing words and behavior from your repertoire of alternatives to best achieve your outcome.
- *Congruence* is being fully aligned with all your internal strategies and behavior. When all your internal systems are fully aligned and in harmony, your words and physiology will match.
- *Integrity* is being whole and complete in terms of your spiritual, emotional, physical, intellectual, and relational aspects. When all these aspects are integrated, your words and behaviors will more likely be consistent with what you value.

Outcomes

A clear outcome is an essential ingredient in communication. Communicating without an outcome is like playing golf without the hole or traveling without a destination. You may end up really enjoying the process or getting to the place you really enjoy, or you may not. Enjoying hitting the ball or your trip is a perfectly good outcome; ending up at the place you want is also productive.

An *outcome* is the result you want, defined in terms of the way you would like to see things happen, what you will hear when you have your outcome, and the way you want to feel. Outcomes are targets that have been clarified and finely honed using five criteria for well-formedness. For an outcome to be viable and well-formed, it must be

- Stated in positive terms
- Demonstrable in sensory experience
- Appropriately specified and contextualized
- Initiated and maintained by an individual and within his or her control
- Ecological, that is, good for all parts of the system

Each of these conditions is elaborated below:

Stated in Positive Terms

An outcome must be stated in positive terms. In conflict situations, you need to be clear about what you want and find out what the other parties want. If you were helping someone arrange furniture and they said to you, "I don't want that chair there," you would not have the information you needed in order to know what to do with the chair. Like the person who doesn't like the position of the chair, people in your school or school district more often know what they don't want. For example, a teacher tells you that she doesn't want to meet with parents after school or a male maintenance employee says that he doesn't like the way the classrooms are kept.

Demonstrable in Sensory Experience

An outcome must be demonstrable in sensory experience to both you and the person with whom you are communicating. For effective communication in a conflict situation, it is critical to specify your outcome(s) and elicit the other parties outcome(s) in terms of what you would need to see, hear, and/or feel in order to know that you have achieved your outcomes. For example, if you and your family decided to have a meeting to plan a vacation, what evidence would demonstrate to you that you had succeeded in meeting your outcome? Would you have a location selected? Would it be written down? Would the details for making arrangements be delegated to specific family members? In conflict situations especially, it is imperative to determine, in advance, the evidence by which success can be measured and recognized.

Appropriately Specified and Contextualized

An outcome needs to be appropriately contextualized and specified. In what contexts do you want it? In what contexts do you not want it? When, where, and with whom do you want it? If a teacher tells you she thinks she deserves compensation for participating on a shared decision-making team that meets after regular school hours and you agree, the appropriate next step is to determine specifically how much compensation, the date the compensation is effective, and the criteria each of you used to reach this conclusion.

Initiated and Maintained by an Individual

An outcome must be one that can be initiated and maintained by an individual. For example, one leadership role of a principal is coaching teachers. In this role, the principal can specifically enable a teacher to make choices to increase personal autonomy. In this way, the welfare of the teacher is maintained by the teacher without the need for the principal's continued assistance.

Coaching is an activity within the principal's control. People often ask for a change in someone else's behavior: "If students would state more specifically what they want" (or "be more responsible," or "be more considerate"), "then I would be more friendly and eager to help them." Although these examples genuinely reflect the student's experience, it is not necessarily within the teacher's control.

Having an experience or behavior initiated and maintained by you assumes that you have the means to achieve the experience or behavior on your own. One possibility in the example referenced above is to assist the teacher by inviting her to remember other times in her life when she chose to be friendly toward people in spite of how they were acting. Once the teacher recalls some time— regardless of how long ago, where, or with whom—you can ask what she did then and whether or not she thinks that behavior might assist her now with the student's difficulty.

Ecological

An outcome must be ecological. Ecology is a branch of biology that deals with the relationship between living organisms and their environments. In relation to human behavior and outcomes, we use the term to remind us that, in order for an outcome to be achieved, it must fit into the totality of our lives and preserve a balance. If an administrator must fill a particular position that necessitates flexible work hours and a potential teacher applicant is bound by certain time constraints (taking classes at a local university, for

1. Stated in the positive
   - What do I want?

2. Demonstrated in sensory experience
   - What would be my evidence that I had achieved my outcome?
   - How would I know if I were getting this outcome?
   - What would I be doing to get it?
   - External Behavior—What would I be seeing and hearing?
   - Internal State—What would I be feeling?
   - Internal Processing—How would I represent this process?
   - What would be a demonstration of it? (Remember you get to see the external behavior here.)

3. Appropriately specified and contextualized
   - Where do I want this outcome?
   - Where do I not want this outcome?
   - When do I want this outcome?
   - With whom do I want this outcome?
   - With whom do I not want this outcome?

4. Initiated and maintained by the individual
   - What resources can I activate to get this outcome?
   - What resources can I acquire to get this outcome?
   - What can I do?
   - What can I begin to do today?
   - What can I continue doing?

5. Ecological
   - What would happen if I got this outcome?
   - How will getting this outcome affect other aspects of my life?
   - How does getting this outcome benefit me/us?
   - Is the positive by-product preserved?

Note: Although these questions are stated in terms of pinpointing your outcome, they can be used by substituting *you* or *we* to elicit the outcomes of others in either an individual or group setting.

Figure 1.4. Questions for Eliciting a Well-Formed Outcome

instance), the outcome of employing this applicant may not be attainable while preserving his or her well-being.

In conflict situations, it is helpful to have some key questions that can be raised to elicit another's outcome. Some of these are identified in Figure 1.4 as a useful reference.

Rapport

Rapport is a shared psychological state between people who are responsive and attentive to each other. Rapport enables increased openness, trust and empathy, and the free flow of communication between people.

Rapport describes a relationship of trust, harmony, affinity, or accord with another. It is a state in which people in communication are attentive and responsive to one another and have a relationship typified by cooperation, agreement, and alignment. Rapport is essential for effective communication and applicable to every communication skill area. Rapport is generally established at both the conscious and unconscious levels by matching some changing element of another's behavior outside his or her conscious awareness. Having rapport with another results in feelings of comfort, satisfaction, and a sense of well-being and shared understanding. Rapport is established through reflective listening and pacing.

The first requirement of effective communication is that rapport be established. It provides a common base from which communication can begin. Rapport is typified by an internal state or feeling that we share some part of a map, world view, or experience of living in a common world. When people are in rapport, feelings of trust and openness are typical. Rapport is a relationship between people in which at least one person has such confidence in the other that he or she is willing to cooperate. Long-term rapport with another requires that you be dependable and follow through on your agreements. Rapport is maintained by assuring that you can be counted on and eliminating or reducing surprises.

Rapport is often thought to be established by using words that indicate agreement and understanding. This normally involves the *content* of a conversation. That is, you need to talk "conservatively" to a conservative and "liberally" to a liberal, or you should learn about a favorite hobby or interest so that you can "share" it. It is true that these may establish a certain commonality of world view, which will have the effect of rapport if you do, in fact, understand and have sympathy with the interest or way of being. However, agreement at the level of *content* is the least effective way for establishing and maintaining rapport. It often imposes the choice of either compromising your integrity or losing the rapport. It has the further disadvantage of requiring that you be in, and stay in, agreement, which doesn't allow for change.

Rapport can be established and maintained at the level of *process* much more easily and powerfully without compromising integrity. Verbally, this means speaking in a way that matches the way the other person understands the world. Nonverbally, it means being a way that matches another's way of being. This includes posture, breathing, gesture, movement, and voice tone. The ways of being in and understanding another's world are the most profound aspect of our experience of the world and therefore create the maximum potential for rapport. Again, long-term rapport requires being totally congruent, behaving in a way that is consistent with your beliefs, and acting with integrity.

Rapport is necessary in communication to achieve your outcome. If you have rapport, you can proceed with the communication. If you don't have it, you need to work on rapport before anything else. If rapport is not present, find a way to establish credibility, continue with establishing rapport, and then proceed with your outcome. The best way to establish rapport is to be truly interested in helping the other achieve his or her outcome.

Trust

Reflective listening and rapport are the gateways to trust. Trust—along with fairness, equity, justice, and integrity—is a foundational ingredient for building quality relationships. Trust is the instinctive, unquestioning belief and confidence in another or yourself. As indicated in Figure 1.5, trust is the intersection between trustworthiness, which is personal, and trusting, which is inter-personal.

Trustworthiness is based on character and competence. Competence is what you can do that is based on your skills. Character is who you are as a person. Competencies are aggregations of skills informed by knowledge and attitudes.

Character is made up of integrity, maturity, and an "abundance mentality" (Covey, 1990). People of integrity are congruent and live what they value; their words match their behavior. Maturity

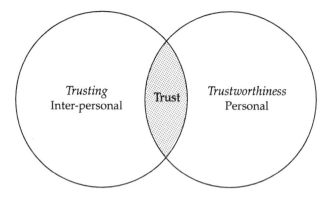

Figure 1.5. Trust: The Intersection Between Trustworthiness and Trusting

involves courage and consideration. An abundance mentality is your view of the world as the glass half full rather than half empty. An abundance mentality reflects the view that there are plenty of resources and goods available for everyone. This mentality is extremely useful in conflict resolution because it opens the door to creative ways of expanding or reconfiguring the pie so that all involved can get their interests met.

Competencies focus knowledge, skills, and attitudes toward the ability to behave in a way that achieves your outcomes. As collections of skills, competencies enable you to achieve your outcomes, deliver on your accountabilities, and maintain high-quality relationships. The skills presented in this book are foundations for the competencies of resolving conflict, facilitating a meeting, and being an effective group member.

Whereas being trustworthy measures your ability to be counted on to live up to your agreements, being trusting measures your ability to rely on the trustworthiness of another. Being trusting, on an inter-personal level, implies letting go of control and enjoying being in rapport with and fully understanding another.

Trust requires clear communication and rapport. It is an essential foundation for learning and inter-personal skill development. We believe that trust is an essential goal for effective inter-personal living and a key in achieving personal autonomy.

Listening and Pacing

School administrators, like most of us, believe they are good listeners or at least capable of good listening. When pressed for specific examples or asked to cite evidence for their claims, they will say that people come to them for advice or they have never been told "you are not listening to me." In addition, most believe that listening is the easiest of the communication skills and that it comes to us naturally without the need for particular attention or training.

In fact, high-quality listening is an acquired skill that can be very sophisticated in practice and powerful in impact, particularly in stressful and conflictual situations. At best, we are only partially successful in its use. Extensive research has demonstrated that in this culture the average listening efficiency (defined as the ability to listen, understand, and retain information) is about 25%. One study reports that 60% of all misunderstandings in business can be traced to poor oral communications (speaking and listening) as opposed to only 1% for written communications (Nichols and Stevens, 1957, p. ix).

An important distinction to explore is the difference between hearing and listening. Hearing does not necessarily connote understanding the meaning of the information the speaker intended to convey. John Drakeford, in his book *The Awesome Power of the Listening Ear,* helps us understand the distinction:

> Hearing is a word used to describe the physiological sensory processes by which auditory sensations are received by the ears and transmitted to the brain. Listening, on the other hand, refers to a more complex psychological procedure involving interpreting and understanding the significance of the sensory experience. (Drakeford, 1967, p. 17)

It is also easy to underestimate the importance of *listening.* In actuality, listening takes up more of our waking hours than any other activity. On the average, we spend between 70% and 80% of our waking moments communicating with others. Of that time, we spend 9% in writing, 16% in reading, 30% in talking, and 45% in listening (Nichols and Stevens, 1957, p. ix).

Listening is central to building and maintaining inter-personal relationships. The quality and effectiveness of our relationships with others, at home or on the job, significantly depend on our ability to listen.

Listening is at the heart of the communication process and is the core, fundamental competency for effective conflict resolution. Listening is critical for school administrators whose success relies on clear, successful communication and the creative, constructive handling of differences. Listening is the key to obtaining and maintaining rapport with another, particularly when that individual is experiencing strong emotion. Listening builds trust and credibility quickly and powerfully because people with strong emotion need and want to be heard and understood. Listening enables understanding in a nonjudgmental, supportive, and respectful manner. In listening, the focus is on the speaker's perspective.

Reflective Listening

Listening is a three-step communication process by which a person gathers information, processes that information, and then forms a hypothesis about what the other person means. Reflective

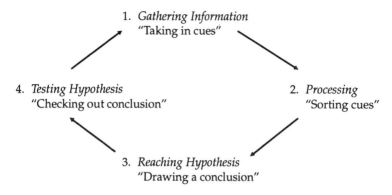

1. *Gathering Information*
   "Taking in cues"

4. *Testing Hypothesis*
   "Checking out conclusion"

2. *Processing*
   "Sorting cues"

3. *Reaching Hypothesis*
   "Drawing a conclusion"

Listening: Steps 1, 2, 3
Reflective Listening: Steps 1, 2, 3, & 4 (Add the 4th step)

Figure 2.1. The Listening Process—An Ongoing Cycle

listening is a four-step communications process in which a person gathers information, processes that information, forms a hypothesis about what the other person means, and then tests the hypothesis with the other person (see Figure 2.1). Listening becomes reflective listening when the fourth step is added.

The purposes of reflective listening are these:

1. To understand what the other person is saying
2. To help the other clarify his or her thoughts and feelings
3. To let the speaker know you have heard and understood
4. To enable the other to clear out strong emotion and allow higher order thinking to take place

Reflective listening is a core skill in communication and conflict resolution. It involves paying respectful attention to the content and feelings expressed in another's communication, hearing and understanding, and then letting the other know your perception of what you heard. In reflective listening you respond actively to another while keeping the focus of your attention totally on the other person. In reflective listening you do not offer your perspective but carefully keep the focus on the other's need or problem. The process consists of two moments:

1. Hearing and understanding what the other person is communicating through words and body language
2. Reflecting (saying to the other) succinctly the thoughts and feelings you heard through your own words, tone of voice, body posture, and gestures, so that the other knows he or she is being heard and understood

Reflective listening is a process of testing your hypothesis or "checking" to verify that you are hearing accurately. In order for this process to be effective, you must be able to perceive accurately what the other is experiencing and communicating; understand the communication at both the content and feeling level; accept the other's feelings; and, if there is a problem, commit to be present to the other while he or she works through that problem and arrives at a solution. When you can answer the question "What is going on with this person right now?" and have that verified, then you are listening reflectively with precision.

Important to reflective listening is testing or checking your hypothesis and verifying that your perception of small segments of another's communication is accurate. Each small segment captures a thought, feeling, or meaning or several thoughts, feelings, or meanings that fit together with a theme or are connected in some way. In reflective listening, you will ordinarily listen to a "bite-size piece" of another's communication and express or state the essence of it to the other in your own words. The checking of another's communication allows you to digest a workable amount of content and feelings. Breaking the conversation down in this way allows both parties in a communication to focus their cognitive abilities on manageable segments of a whole communication. The process of checking the other's communication is illustrated in Figure 2.2.

Your expression or statement to the other provides a check to ensure that you are hearing accurately and clearly and to let the other know that you are understanding what he or she is communicating. Your reflection (statement or expression of this *essence* of a specific chunk of communication) to the other is heard by the other at the unconscious level. If it fits with the speaker's model of the world at that moment, he or she will continue the conversation without a break or say "Yes" or "Exactly" and then continue with

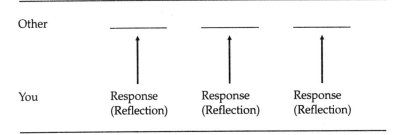

Figure 2.2. "Checking Out" the Communication in Manageable Segments

the communication. If the reflection is somewhat "off target," the speaker will become conscious of the mismatch at the conscious level, experience an interruption, and make the necessary correction. For example, "No, that's not quite right. I think it's more like irritation." If the reflection is completely off target, it diverts the conversation and takes the focus off the speaker.

In using reflective listening skills, you will often literally "break in" to the other's communication. This is experienced as interruptive only if your reflection misses the essence of the other's communication. If your reflection is accurate, the intervention is experienced as facilitative.

A more detailed view of the four steps in the reflective listening process is described in Figure 2.3.

Reflective Listening Examples and Applications

Reflective listening is a vitally important skill for school administrators. As busy people attending to multiple tasks and problems during each hour of the school day, it is essential for administrators to build rapport quickly and effectively, and communicate accurately even under stressful conditions. The "checking out" process provided by reflective listening facilitates an empathic connection between communicators and allows administrators to check the understanding of the many agreements they make for themselves and others. Instead of taking "extra" time out of a very busy school day, the use of reflective listening actually saves time. Establishing rapport allows colleagues and students to get to the heart of the

1. *Taking in cues.* As another communicates, you listen for and record cues in three areas:
   - Content—the content of the communication
   - Feelings—the feelings implied in the communication
   - Context—the external environment surrounding the communication
2. *Processing and sorting out important cues.* Sifting through the cues to arrive at a judgment about what is the essence of a particular "chunk" of the communication.
3. *Reaching a hypothesis/conclusion.* Determining what the essence of the communication is.
4. *Testing/checking your hypothesis with the speaker.* Stating the essence of a "chunk" of the communication to the other in your own words to "check out" whether or not you are understanding the other.

Figure 2.3. Four Steps in Reflective Listening

matter more easily and diminishes the chance of misunderstanding around perceptions and agreements. When reflective listening is used in problem solving, others are empowered. Such empowerment enables critical stakeholders to solve their own problems, thereby freeing administrators from dependency relationships. And, of course, reflective listening is a key contributor to success in managing conflict so that productive negotiation can take place.

Some examples of reflective listening responses are illustrated in the four situations in Figure 2.4. These examples are instances in which reflective listening is used as the first response to enter the speaker's world and establish rapport quickly and efficiently. Frequently, this initial reflection will be followed by more reflections, pacing, and perhaps problem solving and negotiation.

Some specific contexts in which reflective listening is useful include the following:

- Helping another clear out negative emotion when experiencing a difficulty or problem
- Solving problems and managing agreements
- Creating a climate of warmth and responsiveness
- Handling resistance or anger
- Settling disputes and differences, including conflict management and negotiation

Situation 1:

These meetings continually last an hour or more over the allotted time, and I can't take that kind of time.

You might say:

- You feel frustrated when meetings last beyond the time scheduled.

Situation 2:

I made several good suggestions at the faculty committee meeting, but no one seemed to pay any attention to them. It was as if I didn't say anything at all.

You might say:

- You feel discounted when no one pays attention to your ideas.

Situation 3:

Our decision-making process isn't working. The people just don't follow the steps they agreed to.

You might say:

- You're feeling upset when people don't keep their commitments.

Situation 4:

My interview for the principal's job really went well. I think I'm sure to land the position.

You might say:

- You feel confident about the interview and your job prospects.

Figure 2.4. Examples of Reflective Listening Responses

- Leading or participating in group discussion and dialogue.
- Clarifying directions

Reflective listening offers a number of significant benefits. Reflective listening

- Lets the other person realize he or she has been heard, understood, cared for, and supported
- Provides the other with information about what he or she said
- Allows you to check your own accuracy in hearing what the other has said

- Avoids the illusion of understanding
- Helps the other focus on self, ventilate, sort out issues, express feelings, and deal more effectively with emotions
- Facilitates the movement to problem solving
- Clarifies what you are expected to do

When to Reflective-Listen

Reflective listening is facilitated when the following conditions are present:

- The other person has the stronger need to be heard and the greater emotional energy.
- You have, and choose to take, the time to listen.
- You can remain reasonably separate and objective and not become personally involved in what the other is saying or react with a defensive response.
- You trust the resourcefulness of the other person to be responsible for his or her own life.

Reactive Responses

Reactive responses in listening situations are statements that interfere with the other's ability to express clear meaning. They are likely to take the focus off the other. Because a key element of listening is enabling the other to focus on his or her thoughts and feelings, a reactive response is inhibiting. The communication process is often frustrated and blocked when the listener allows reactive responses, which are particularly inappropriate when the other has a strong need or a problem or is experiencing strong emotion about an issue. Reactive responses tend to

- Serve the need of the responder and not the speaker
- Have a "high risk" of taking the focus off the speaker
- Tend to make the speaker feel judged, stupid, or unimportant

Reactive responses can be grouped into the following three categories:

1. *Solving:* sidetracking the other person's communication by moving right away to a solution offered by you. Your questions, advice, ordering, threatening, moralizing, or problem solving often interfere with the other person's ability to explore those thoughts and feelings that can lead to solutions that address the heart of the situation. Using responses in this category communicates the subtle message, "You're too dumb to figure this out so I will tell you." Some of these solving responses might be more appropriate when the speaker has finished expressing the issue and needs help or when the speaker has finished whatever he or she wanted to say. Threatening and moralizing responses are never useful.

2. *Evaluating/Judging:* changing the focus of the conversation by shifting it from the other's concerns to your own diagnosis, interpretation, judgment, or praise of the other person or agreement or disagreement with him or her. The subtle message sent in this category is "There's something the matter with you."

3. *Withdrawing:* distracting the other person from his or her agenda, often by reassuring the other that everything will be all right or diverting to another agenda. The subtle message conveyed by the responder in this category is "I'm really uncomfortable hearing these feelings."

By taking the focus off the other, reactive responses are very likely to do the following:

- Derail the conversation
- Block the other person from finding the solution to his or her problem
- Lower the other person's self-esteem
- Distance you from the other
- Diminish the other person's motivation and initiative

These responses tend to have the effect of decreasing contact with the other and blocking the other from saying more because they tend to imply a desire to change or modify the other person, take responsibility away from the other, cause resentment or defensiveness, and evoke a negative or aggressive response.

Category	Example	Consequences/Effects

Solving
Listener offering
  solutions pre-
  maturely and/or
  imappropriately
	1. Ordering
	2. Threatening*
	3. Moralizing*
	4. Advising
	5. Questioning
	6. Problem
	   Solving
		• Reduces autonomy
		  of speaker
		• Inhibits exploration
		  of problem

Evaluating/Judging
Listener drawing
  conclusions about
  speaker's intention
	7. Agreeing/
	   Disagreeing
	8. Diagnosing
	9. Criticizing/
	   Blaming*
	10. Praising
	   (Judgmental)
		• Blocks speaker from
		  moving forward
		• Judges speaker as
		  person

Withdrawing
Listener avoiding
  speaker's concerns/
  feelings
	11. Logical Arguing
	12. Understanding*
	13. Reassuring
	14. Diverting*
		• Disengages listener
		• Shuts down speaker

* Never useful

Figure 2.5. Categories and Examples of Reactive Responses

Figure 2.5 presents the three categories of reactive responses and lists examples. All reactive responses tend to take the focus off the other—those marked with an asterisk are never useful. The following are illustrations of the examples of typical reactive responses:

Solving

1. *Ordering*

Telling the other person to do something.

- You must do this by Friday.
- You can't do it that way.
- I expect you to do this.
- Stop it.

2. *Threatening**

Telling the other person what negative consequences will occur if he or she does something; sometimes alluding to the use of force.

- You had better do this, or else!
- If you don't do it, then . . .
- You'd better not try that . . .
- I warn you, if you do that . . .

3. *Moralizing**

Telling the other person why he or she *should* or *ought to* do something.

- You really should do this by Friday.
- You ought to try.
- You ought to do this; it's your duty.
- This is something I really urge you to do.

4. *Advising*

Telling the other person how to solve his or her problem.

- Let me suggest . . .
- It would be best for you if . . .
- If I were you, I'd . . .
- The best solution is . . .

5. *Questioning*

Trying to find reasons, facts, motives, causes, or information that will help you solve the other person's problem (closed-ended questions).

- Why did you do that?
- What have you done to solve it?
- Have you consulted anyone?
- Who has influenced you?

6. *Problem Solving*

Engaging the other in a problem-solving process prematurely (facilitating a problem-solving process with another is often appropriate after listening first).

- Let's solve this problem now . . .
- We have to be rational about this . . .
- Maybe if we brainstorm some alternatives now . . .
- Let's set aside these feelings and address the real issues . . .

Evaluating/Judging

7. Agreeing/Disagreeing

Making a judgment of another's communication by agreeing or disagreeing with him or her.

- I agree . . . (I disagree . . .)
- Yes.
- You're absolutely right.
- You're all wrong on that point.

8. Diagnosing

Telling the other person what his or her motives are or analyzing the "whys" behind what he or she is doing or saying (communicating that you have figured out, or diagnosed, the other).

- You're saying this because you are angry.
- What you really need is . . .
- You have problems with authority.
- You want to look good.

9. Criticizing/Blaming*

Making the other person feel stupid, outcast, or foolish (stereotyping or categorizing).

- You're out of line.
- You didn't do it right.
- You are a fuzzy thinker.
- It's your fault.

10. Praising

Offering a positive evaluation or judgment (often manipulative and/or condescending, sometimes sarcastic).

- You usually have such good judgment.
- You have so much potential.
- You've made quite a bit of progress.

Note: Praising has a powerful and important role in building autonomy when appropriately offered. Praising is a reactive response only when a judgment is made about the other's behavior. The syntax of "You must be feeling good about ———" reinforces productive behavior and is useful.

Withdrawing

11. *Logical Arguing*

Trying to divert the other person from his or her feelings with facts, arguments, logic, information, or expert opinions that happen to agree with your own.

- The facts are in favor of . . .
- Let me give you the facts.
- Here is the right way.

12. *Understanding**

Trying to let the person know you understand by telling him or her directly (saying the words "I understand").

- I understand.
- I understand totally what you are saying.
- I understand just how you're feeling.
- I understand just what you're thinking.

13. *Reassuring*

Trying to make the other person feel better; trying to either talk the other out of his or her feelings (making the feelings go away) or deny the strength of the feelings.

- Things will get better.
- It's always darkest before the dawn.
- Every cloud has a silver lining.
- It's not that bad.

14. *Diverting**

Trying to get the other person away from the problem or getting away from it yourself. Trying to change the focus by kidding, offering other things to do, or pushing the problem away.

- Think about the positive side.
- Try not to worry about it until you've tried it.
- Let's have lunch and forget about it.
- That reminds me of the time when . . .

All the reactive responses have the potential of taking the focus off the other person's agenda and increasing their emotional energy in ways that inhibit effective problem solving. Reactive responses need to be identified in intense listening situations and avoided. You need to reflectively listen to others instead.

Reactive Response Dialogue

Here is a hypothetical dialogue to help illuminate some of the potential negative effects of reactive responses. The dialogue illustrates the use of each example reactive response where a reflective listening response would be more appropriate.

A school principal (Kevin) and one of the teachers (Emily) are having a discussion in his office after school. Emily has had a terrible day. One of her daughters called to say that she got sick at school and missed her final exams, her fifth-grade students were disruptive in class in anticipation of the school vacation, and one of her students' parents had called her blaming her for something she had not done. To top it off, her social studies curriculum team got into a big argument, and two members who had not been working effectively threatened to quit, even though the work wasn't done. Emily was the accountable person for the curriculum report due in three days.

Emily initiates the discussion:

Emily: You won't believe the day I've had. It's one of the worst days I've had here. And that curriculum committee is too much. I'll never get the report done.

Kevin: (*Ordering—Commanding the other to do something*) Now Emily, just pull yourself together. Tell your colleagues to shape up and finish the report. The assistant superintendent is waiting for it.

Emily: I know. But there's no way we can get it done.

Kevin: (*Threatening—Using the specter of negative consequences to get the other to do something*) If you don't get it done by Friday, it's you who is going to be in trouble. The assistant superintendent is not a patient person.

Emily: At this point I really don't care.

Kevin: (*Moralizing—Telling the other why she ought to do something*) Don't care! Why Emily, you surprise me. If we all took that attitude this school system would be in a terrible mess. We're part of a team here, and you just need to pick up the pieces for the others on your committee.

Emily: Well, there's no way I can do this task alone by Friday, and the others are hardly speaking to one another.

Kevin: (*Advising—Telling the other how to solve the problem*) Now Emily, I've tried to tell you not to take any nonsense from these teachers. If I were you, I'd crack the whip and tell them to grow up and act their age.

Emily: If I said that, then they would all turn against me. They already think I'm riding them too hard.

Kevin: (*Questioning—Through close-ended questions, eliciting reasons, motives, or facts to allow listener to solve other's problem quickly or put blame on speaker*) Why do you think you're so soft on them? Is it because they are so much older than you? Are you intimidated by people who have been here longer than you have?

Emily: That's nonsense. It's not their age or anything personal. They just won't do the work to get the task done.

Kevin: (*Problem Solving—Solving problem prematurely, cutting short the necessary exploration of the problem*) Let's solve this right now. Tomorrow morning, go in and demand they give you the report within 24 hours.

Emily: I don't know if that will work at this point. They're not even talking to each other right now.

Kevin: (*Agreeing/Disagreeing—Agreeing/disagreeing with other's conclusions or assessment*) You're absolutely wrong to let them carry on like this.

Emily: Well, I really don't know what else to do.

Kevin: (*Diagnosing—Telling other what her motives are or analyzing the "whys" behind behavior or words*) You're just down in the dumps because your husband got laid off. I'm sure you're depressed and worried and you're bringing those attitudes into your work here. You're so negative these days.

Emily: That's not true! I come to work eager to work with my students and colleagues. It's just that these bozos aren't holding up their end and are acting like two-year-olds!

Kevin: (*Criticizing/Blaming—Stereotyping or categorizing the person as a way to diminish her concerns*) I think it really might be your fault. You're such a naive idealist, always thinking the world is fair and everyone will do their share. I don't know who fed you that baloney.

Emily: Oh, that's just great. We should all go around and pick up for the slackers. I should do all the work and they should all get the credit.

Kevin: (*Praising—Offering a nonspecific, positive judgment that is often condescending and manipulative and sometimes sarcastic*) Well, that's the way it is sometimes. You've always been one who's willing to go the extra mile for the good of the school. It sure would be good to have you come through again for us.

Emily: Well, I'll try, but I don't think it will work this time. And I'm angry about always having to cover up for them.

Kevin: (*Logical Arguing—Trying to divert the other from her feelings with facts or information to agree with your solution*) Let's look at the facts here. These teachers are making darn good money to meet their responsibilities, and one of those responsibilities is to do committee work. You certainly have the right to demand more from them.

Emily: Maybe you do have a point. But with everything going on in my life right now, I sure didn't need this problem with the curriculum committee.

Kevin: (*Understanding—Using the proper words but not giving evidence of understanding*) I understand just how you feel.

Emily: I don't think you do. You don't have to work with them on this project. I'll never get it done on time doing it all myself.

Kevin: (*Reassuring—Trying to make the other feel better by denying the strength of her feelings*) Don't worry. You'll get it done one way or another and this crisis will pass. Maybe the others will surprise you and come through.

Emily: I doubt it—and I'm still worried and frustrated.

Kevin: (*Diverting—Trying to get you and the other away from the problem by changing the focus*) Let's forget it and go to the lounge for coffee. I can tell you about the new boat I just bought.

Even though reactive responses are usually well-intentioned and are habitual in most of us, we need to recognize that they have damaging costs: They take the focus off the other's thoughts and feelings and do not enable them to become more resourceful. In addition, they send subtle messages to the other person. They say, "You are not OK as you are." Reactive responses need to be recognized and avoided, especially in times when one or more of the parties have high energy and a high need to be listened to and understood. On these occasions, use reflective listening instead of reactive responses to help clarify thoughts, work constructively with feelings, and move toward problem solving if necessary.

Laser Listening

Laser listening moves beyond reflective listening to testing or checking out not only what the person is saying but what he or she is implying. It is adapted from Gerard Egan's work on advanced accurate empathy (Egan, 1976). Such a communication offers others an external, perhaps more objective, frame of reference so that they can see themselves more clearly.

Laser listening focuses the speaker on the theme and implications underlying the communication. With this focus, the speaker is enabled to discover possible meanings that might otherwise be totally outside his or her awareness.

At the heart of laser listening are the skills of reflective listening and sensory acuity. Laser listening communicates that you, the listener, are deeply connected with the other. The following illustrates the difference between reflective listening and laser listening:

Teacher: I just don't seem to be able to fit into the teaching team. I try as hard as any of you to be a part, but I can't seem to make friends very easily. It's probably my own fault, but my attempts don't work out. I don't know what more to do.

A reflective listening response might be:

It's frustrating for you to try so hard with your colleagues and not seem to get anywhere.

A laser listening response might be:

You seem concerned about being with people and groups generally.

The laser listening response tends to name the implication or the deeper structure of the communication. To uncover an appropriate laser listening response, ask yourself, "What is the underlying issue here?" or "What is the vague issue that could be made clear?" Although with laser listening you interpret what another person says or does, your interpretation is based on the information the other person has provided, both verbal and nonverbal.

Laser listening is not a one-way process. The purpose of using laser listening is to help uncover meaning, clarify issues, and improve relationships between individuals and within groups.

Pacing

Pacing is a powerful process by which you can establish and maintain rapport. It is a mirrorlike matching of another's experience, through matching some changing element of another's physiology outside the other's conscious awareness. Pacing emphasizes the importance of acknowledging aspects of the other person's behavior, thereby meeting the other person at his or her model of the world. You simply utilize the other person's own behavior to establish and maintain rapport.

Pacing begins by recognizing that people are always communicating and do so in systematic ways. Therefore, behavior you can identify you can pace, by adjusting your own behavior (nonverbal and verbal) to move with the other person. Using pacing to establish rapport suggests to the other: "I am like you," "We are in sync," "You can trust me." Pacing allows you to make contact with the other's model of the world and to establish rapport at an unconscious level. Pacing is joining the other's reality in a particular moment.

Pacing tends to minimize differences and accentuate similarities so that the perception of understanding is increased and maintained. You can pace any changing element of another's behavior. Some of the more dominant possibilities are elaborated as follows:

- *Body Posture:* Matching body posture is the easiest but also the most obvious way to pace. To avoid detection, more subtle matching of body posture, such as a tilt of the head or a shift of a hand position, is more effective than a gross body similarity such as matching crossed legs precisely.
- *Movement:* Matching movement is an effective pacing technique, especially when the rhythm of the movement is matched with another movement such as matching a head nod with a hand movement. Hand and arm movements can also be matched, but only when it's your turn to speak.
- *Voice Patterns:* Matching voice tone, tempo, and timbre is probably the most effective pacing technique, primarily because most people are somewhat unaware of their voice patterns. Matching tempo is probably the easiest to use without being noticed. If another is angry and speaks in a loud, fast voice, you will need to join the other's reality by matching the voice volume and rate to get rapport.
- *Breathing Pattern:* Matching the breathing rate and place in the chest when the other is inhaling air.
- *Language:* Matching the significant words of the other that seem to have special meaning to him or her.

Mastering pacing will enable you to establish rapport with whomever you choose. It is extremely important to be graceful and respectful in your pacing so that what you are doing does not come

1. Identify the internal state the other person is experiencing.

2. Pace some changing element of the other's behavior.

3. Select some element of behavior to lead.

4. Alter your behavior (gently) to test rapport or elicit a desired state.

Figure 2.6. Four Steps in the Pacing Process

into the conscious awareness of the other person. You want to avoid mimicking the other's behavior exactly.

The four steps in the pacing process, including the leading steps for checking the level of rapport, are listed in Figure 2.6.

Leading

Leading is done to test rapport or elicit a desired state. In order to lead you select a specific behavior you have been pacing (for example, auditory volume) and then you alter your behavior (for instance, increase or decrease the volume). When someone responds by following you (by increasing or decreasing their volume) within 30 to 90 seconds, a successful lead has been accomplished. If your outcome for leading is to test rapport and the individual follows you, it is a signal that you can now gather or present information. When your outcome is to elicit a desired state and the individual follows your lead, you continue pacing and leading until you can see and hear external cues indicating the desired state is present.

Pacing and leading are patterns that are evident in almost everything we do. They are usually outside our conscious awareness. Pacing, in essence, is sharing the other person's behavioral reality. What automatically develops as a result of graceful pacing is high-level rapport and trust with the other person.

The only time pacing should not be used is if you are trying to decrease rapport. Leading evokes a change in the other person's behavior in the direction of the outcome you want. Pacing and leading work hand in hand. Without the ability to lead the other person into new behavior, pacing might be ineffective in producing the outcome you want. You must know your intended outcome in order to know when to pace and when to lead.

Chunking and Problem Solving

The Conflict Resolution Model referenced in the introduction to this book and described in *Conflict Resolution: Building Bridges* involves conflict management and negotiation. Figure 3.1 illustrates this Conflict Resolution Model, differentiating the stages of conflict management and negotiation. Two important concepts are listed in the negotiation stage: chunking and problem solving. *Chunking* is an essential skill for differentiating positions and interests. *Problem solving* is a framework for bridging differences in a conflict situation. The skill of chunking and the problem-solving model are illustrated in this chapter.

Chunking

Chunking is the altering of logical levels in communication. Logical level can also be thought of as levels of generality or abstraction. You can *chunk up*, moving from a specific example to a more general concept. You can *chunk down*, moving from a general concept to a specific example. Chunking up is used to determine the positive intention behind behavior or what you want. The positive intention is the interest behind someone's position.

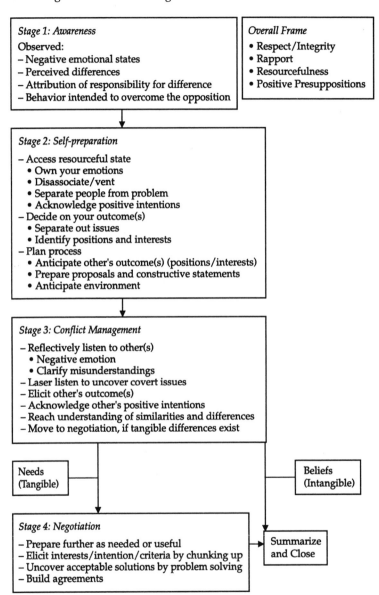

Stage 1: *Awareness*
Observed:
– Negative emotional states
– Perceived differences
– Attribution of responsibility for difference
– Behavior intended to overcome the opposition

Overall Frame
• Respect/Integrity
• Rapport
• Resourcefulness
• Positive Presuppositions

Stage 2: *Self-preparation*
– Access resourceful state
  • Own your emotions
  • Disassociate/vent
  • Separate people from problem
  • Acknowledge positive intentions
– Decide on your outcome(s)
  • Separate out issues
  • Identify positions and interests
– Plan process
  • Anticipate other's outcome(s) (positions/interests)
  • Prepare proposals and constructive statements
  • Anticipate environment

Stage 3: *Conflict Management*
– Reflectively listen to other(s)
  • Negative emotion
  • Clarify misunderstandings
– Laser listen to uncover covert issues
– Elicit other's outcome(s)
– Acknowledge other's positive intentions
– Reach understanding of similarities and differences
– Move to negotiation, if tangible differences exist

Needs
(Tangible)

Beliefs
(Intangible)

Stage 4: *Negotiation*
– Prepare further as needed or useful
– Elicit interests/intention/criteria by chunking up
– Uncover acceptable solutions by problem solving
– Build agreements

Summarize
and Close

Figure 3.1. The Conflict Resolution Model (elaborated version)

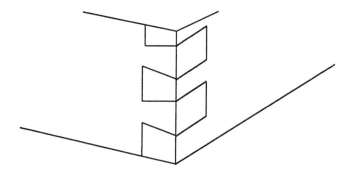

Figure 3.2. Dovetailing Interests

This chunking concept is used in negotiation. Negotiation usually requires dovetailing or trading interests. Dovetailing involves "fitting together" the interests of the parties in a mutually acceptable solution. This concept emerges from cabinetmaking and refers to a particular way of joining two boards together—a dovetail joint, as shown in Figure 3.2. Dovetailing people's interests enables their satisfaction. If all parties can see their interests satisfied, movement toward the resolution of a conflict is substantially enhanced.

Chunking is usually used in negotiation to facilitate the mutual discovery of interests behind positions. As previously indicated, a position is a particular solution you want and an interest is why you want that solution.

If an initial position can be chunked up or made more general, the opportunity to uncover interests that can be dovetailed or fit together is increased. An example of differentiating position from interests is the following case of the 5-week grading reports:

The high school teachers were in conflict about the 5-week progress reports. One group (Party A) insisted that they were an unnecessary inconvenience that took valuable time away from course preparation. They wanted the report requirement abolished. The other group (Party B) was equally certain in their position that the 5-week reports were necessary and wanted the status quo to prevail. Their view was that the reports, plus the form they had all been using for the reports, must continue as is.

The positions, or predetermined solutions, of the parties were as follows:

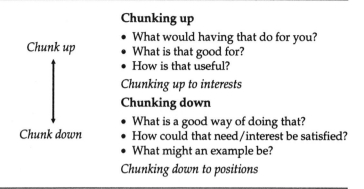

Figure 3.3. Chunking Questions

Party A: Abolish the 5-week reports.
Party B: Continue the report requirement without change.

A compromise might be changing the timing of the reports from 5 weeks to 7 weeks or shortening the report form. These solutions would likely result in some form of resentment on both sides. Instead of compromise, the parties decided a collaborative outcome was wiser and entered into a process to achieve an outcome satisfactory to both parties. Each group first identified its own interests and elicited the interests of the other group.

The process of identifying your interests or eliciting interests from another is greatly facilitated by asking the primary *chunking-up* question to move from positions to interests:

What would having that (the position) do for you?

This question and alternative similar questions for chunking up from positions to interests are illustrated in Figure 3.3.

Each party used the chunking-up question to identify its interests and the interests of the other party. Their interests were

Party A's Interests

- Use time productively and have time to prepare for classes.
- Give students effective feedback on progress.
- Have choices about method of feedback to provide students.

Party B's Interests

- Use time efficiently.
- Give students effective feedback on progress.
- Ensure every teacher is communicating with students and parents.

After eliciting and considering their collective interests, the parties agreed to brainstorm some ideas to attempt to meet all of their interests. Brainstorming is a way of *chunking down*. It is facilitated by the chunking-down question:

What are some ways of satisfying our collective interests? (See Figure 3.3 for additional chunking-down questions)

In responding to this question, the parties identified several ideas:

1. Use some kind of feedback mechanism after the first 5 weeks of the semester.
2. Revise the form so that it is less time-consuming without sacrificing the utility of the feedback.
3. Allow teachers the options of face-to-face meetings with student and parents or three-way telephone conversations (with use of the school speaker phone system).

Both parties were happy with the options and agreed to revising the form and allowing flexibility in reporting at a 5-week period. This solution met their collective interests without having to compromise on something important to them. They then developed an action plan to put their solution into practice. No feelings of resentment remained for either party.

Problem Solving

School administrators solve problems many times during their workday. Most of the time they do this on "automatic pilot"; that is, they just make a decision and solve the problem without think-

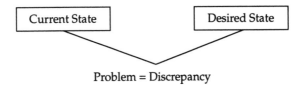

Problem = Discrepancy

The difference between the current state
and the desired future state.

Figure 3.4. Problem Definition

ing of the particular process they used. However, some problems
are more complex and difficult and would benefit by a more elabo-
rate and structured process. In this section, a problem-solving process
is introduced that we have found valuable in conflict resolution.
The problem-solving model maximizes the chances for uncovering
creative and "doable" solutions. Administrators will find many
opportunities to use this model, whether working on their own
problems, helping another solve his or her problem, facilitating
group problems, or using it as part of an overall negotiation strategy with another party.

Problem solving is a process of identifying a discrepancy between a current and a desired state and working out the steps required to reach that desired state. Thus a problem is the difference
between these two states. Figure 3.4 illustrates this definition
graphically.

The current state is where you are in the present moment—a
snapshot of the situation now. The desired state is where you want
to be. In facilitating a problem-solving process for another, the current state is where the other person is right now. The desired state
is where he or she wants to be. Some examples are indicated in
Figure 3.5.

In the first case illustrated in Figure 3.5, the other wishes to move
from a state of smoking cigarettes to a desired future state of non-
smoking. The problem is the discrepancy, or the smoking behavior.
In the second case, the other wishes to get school budgets completed on time. The discrepancy in this case is the work not done
on time.

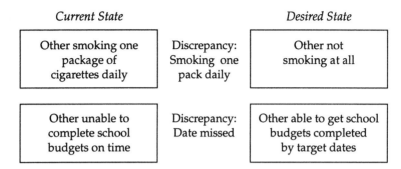

Figure 3.5. Examples of Problem as Discrepancy

The process for collapsing the differences between the current and desired states is problem solving. The seven-step problem-solving process presented in this chapter is a universal model for a variety of contexts:

- Solving an internal discrepancy within yourself
- Helping another with a discrepancy
- Working out solutions to group problems either as a facilitator and/or group member
- Negotiating a solution to a problem between you and another

The generic problem-solving process is outlined in Figure 3.6 and the steps in the process are described in detail in Steps 1-7. These seven steps focus on developing the solution—the problem is solved when the planned solution is implemented. The two future-action steps are the implementation steps. As an administrator, you will find many opportunities to use this model in helping another solve a problem by increasing the other's autonomy, helping a group solve a problem, or solving a problem between you and another. The steps are described below in the context of using the process to assist another with his or her problem.

Step 1: Define the Problem

Define the problem in terms of the other's needs, as he or she expressed them in the reflective-listening process. Asking the fol-

1. Define the problem in terms of desired state (results, needs).
2. Identify all options for solution and clarify options that are ambiguous (brainstorm).
3. Evaluate alternative solutions.
4. Decide on an acceptable solution (one option or combination of options).
5. Develop an implementation/action plan (who will do what by when).
6. Develop a process for evaluating the results (include in implementation/ action plan).
7. Talk about the experience (of problem solving).

Future Actions
1. Implement the solution.
2. Evaluate the result.

Figure 3.6. The Problem-Solving Process (Katz & Lawyer, 1985)

lowing questions is often helpful in helping another understand the discrepancy:

- What is the current state and why is that problematic or troublesome?
- What is the desired state or desired result expressed in terms of needs or interests? (Concrete behaviors—preferably see, hear, feel description of desired state)
- What is the discrepancy between the two states?

Given that the problem is a discrepancy between a current state and a desired state, it is useful in problem solving to express the problem in terms of needs and interests underlying the desired future state or result. This can be done by stating the problem as a "How to . . . " statement, using the following formula:

"How to _____   _____"
        (Action Verb)   (Desired Result)

Through reflective listening, you eventually reach the point where you can say, "It looks like we need to figure out how to . . . "

Verb	*Result*
"How to . . . learn	effective conflict resolution skills."
"How to . . . receive	the support of my superintendent."
"How to . . . get	a budget increase of 10%."
"How to . . . plan	for the high school graduation ceremony."

Figure 3.7. Example "How to . . . " Statements

This statement will take the current and desired states into consideration but will be presented in terms of the desired state or result (where the other wants to be). It must be a specific and practical statement that will clarify the discrepancy and be the first step in moving toward its resolution. Some examples of "How to . . . " statements are listed in Figure 3.7.

Always make the "How to . . . " statement positive, not negative. For example:

- Negative: "How to stop overeating"
- Positive: "How to eat in a way that meets your nutritional requirements and maintains your weight between 120 and 125 pounds"

Another important aspect of the "How to . . . " statement is to make it as specific and concrete as possible. For example:

- Too general: "How to lose weight"
- More specific: "How to get my weight to 165 pounds"

A third important aspect of the "How to . . . " statement is to be concise and to the point. For example:

- Too long and confusing: "How to get back on the right track and try and start studying so I can feel confident that I can pass my dissertation defense, so I'll graduate in May like I have been planning for four years"
- More concise: "How to defend my doctoral dissertation successfully by April 15th"

A simple example illustrating how to formulate a problem-solving statement would be a male school administrator who is constantly late with reports for the school board. His tardiness causes board members to be ill-prepared to discuss important issues, and their frustration comes out in sarcastic comments to the administrator, which embarrasses him in front of his peers. The desired state is for the administrator to have his reports attractively and accurately prepared and delivered to board members prior to the meeting so that they can digest the information and be ready to discuss important issues in a pleasant manner. The problem, in simple terms, is that the board reports are not prepared and delivered in advance. Wording the problem in terms of the desired state will allow a full exploration of the problem in terms of the underlying interests. Using the "How to . . . " syntax, the problem statement might read:

"How to ensure (Action Verb) that reports are prepared and delivered to board members prior to the board meeting so that discussion of important issues can take place" (Desired Result— expressed in terms of needs and interest).

Step 2: Identify Options for a Solution

Once the problem is clearly defined, you can brainstorm to generate options that may resolve the discrepancy and enable the other to reach his or her desired state. In this step, the stakeholders need to assess the feasibility and attractiveness of each option and whether implementing the option will help them progress toward the future state.

Brainstorming is the surfacing of alternatives without judging or evaluating them. It is very important that you involve all the stakeholders in this brainstorming process. It is useful to actually write the options on paper so that each of the parties can see as well as hear the list of possible solutions. In brainstorming, in order to encourage creativity and imagination, it is important not to evaluate any of the ideas. Clarify any options that might be ambiguous. Evaluation will take place in Step 3.

Step 3: Evaluate Alternative Solutions

This step should be clearly separated from Step 2, in order that every option may be carefully considered. Combining Steps 2 and 3 may cause a viable solution to be written off before it is fully explored. It is also imperative that the other is involved in evaluating all the options. It is both more effective and respectful for you to help the other decide on his or her own solution, as opposed to giving the other the solution to the problem.

It is important to have the "How to . . . " statement visible during this step, because the situation depicted in the desired state serves as criteria with which to judge the effectiveness of the options. Step 3 might be viewed as a "first cut" to decide which option or combination of options will help you move toward the desired state.

Step 4: Decide on an Acceptable Solution

After full evaluation of each option, the other must decide which is best for him or her. There may be financial, time, lifestyle, or other variables that need to be considered before he or she makes a decision. If you are facilitating this process with another party, only he or she knows which options are acceptable. The process is more effective when the person experiencing the problem decides on his or her own solution. If you provide the other with the answer to the problem, the likelihood of a successful follow-through is diminished.

This step gives the other an opportunity to more carefully evaluate the merits of each option in relationship to achieving the desired state and his or her willingness and ability to implement the options. One or more options might be selected at this time. Many times, options will be sequential in nature, so that it will make sense to select several options that are in effect steps toward an overall strategy.

Step 5: Develop an Implementation/Action Plan

In this step, specificity is important. Now that an option or combination of options has been chosen, a number of things must be clearly specified:

- What are the steps needed to arrive at the solution?
- Who is responsible for each step?
- What resources are needed (for instance, money, time)?
- How long will it take (what is the target date for each step)?

It is also helpful to summarize what has been decided to ensure that every aspect of the solution has been carefully considered and is clearly understood. This is a very important step in the problem-solving process. Without a specific, well-thought-out action plan, options are merely good ideas. They need to be translated into steps for constructive action to make a difference in achieving the desired state.

Step 6: Develop a Process for Evaluating Results

This step involves building into the implementation plan a time and process for evaluating the results. Specific times must be set up to give the other an opportunity to talk about how the implementation plan is working. Such monitoring enables new problems to be addressed and any new variables considered. A final evaluation should take into account the entire effort.

Step 7: Talk About the Experience

After the implementation plan has been set up, you might invite the other to discuss his or her thoughts and feelings about the process, using some of the following questions as a guide:

- Does the other feel comfortable with the plan?
- Does the other understand all the aspects?
- How does the other feel about the problem-solving process they have just gone through?

This last step in the problem-solving process (talking about the experience) is important. A smooth close will encourage positive feelings in the other; an awkward close may stir negative feelings and reduce commitment to the implementation plan itself. It is important to summarize and to ensure the other that you will be available if any difficulties should arise—if you have, and are willing, to take the time. Talking about the experience will hopefully bring out uncomfortable feelings and surface any remaining obstacles that might jeopardize the implementation plan. Always present yourself as caring, friendly, easy to talk to, and helpful to the person solving the problem.

This problem-solving process produces an appropriate action plan for attending to the problem. Future-action steps include implementing the solution and evaluating the results in accordance with the implementation/action plan.

The essence of the seven-step problem-solving process is allowing those closely affected by the problem to take the responsibility for defining the problem and selecting options to try to solve it. It is both more effective and more respectful for the listener to help the other generate his or her own solution rather than to propose whatever solution might appear appropriate from the listener's viewpoint. Among the reasons for this are these:

- The other has more of the pertinent information about the problem—past, present, and future.
- The other has to implement the solution, not you as the listener.
- The other takes all the risks.
- The other's self-confidence is fostered when he or she assumes responsibility for developing and implementing the solution.
- The other's feeling of independence is fostered when he or she takes responsibility for the problem, decides on an appropriate solution, and implements the action plan.

Guidelines for using the seven-step problem-solving model are included in Figure 3.8.

In a negotiation situation, at least one other party is involved. In this case, the interests of all the parties must be uncovered and a "How to . . . " statement formulated that encompasses all the interests. Once the "How to . . . " statement is agreed to by all the parties, the seven-step problem-solving process can be used to develop a solution that is acceptable to all the parties.

1. Define the problem in terms of the interests of both parties:
   - State the problem in a way that does not communicate blame or judgment.
   - Test out the problem statement and gain acceptance.
   - Maintain rapport at all times.
   - Reflective-listen to the other.
   - Be sure you understand the other's interests and be ready to clarify yours, as needed.
2. Identify (and clarify) all possible options for a solution:
   - Ask the other to suggest possible solutions.
   - Use reflective listening; treat the other's ideas with respect.
   - Discourage evaluation until a number of possible options have been proposed.
3. Evaluate alternative solutions:
   - Be honest.
   - Use reflective listening.
   - Be open to new options and modifications that come to mind.
   - Test any likely options to make sure they satisfy both parties' interests.
4. Decide on an acceptable solution:
   - Don't push or impose a solution on the other.
   - When a decision appears close, state this so that both understand it.
5. Develop an implementation/action plan:
   - Decide specifically who does what and when.
6. Develop a process for evaluating results:
   - Incorporate this process into the implementation plan.
7. Talk about the experience:
   - Invite the other to share perspectives on the process.
   - Share your own perspectives on the process.

Figure 3.8. Guidelines for Using the Seven-Step Problem-Solving Model

Referral/Transferal

As the problem or issue is defined and explored, and the other person wishes for or expects certain assistance from you, it may become apparent that his or her need is one that could more appropriately be dealt with by some trained individual or agency other than yourself. In such instances, you need to skillfully refer or transfer the person to whomever is capable of providing the needed assistance:

- Referral of a person involves broadening and sharing (not transferring) the responsibility for providing help. In referral, you are not turning the person over to another party; you remain the person's primary support, but with another skilled party in collaboration.
- Transferal of a person involves taking steps to shift the responsibility for providing care and assistance from yourself to another skilled party.

A basic insight is to accept referral/transferal as an integral part of the helping process, for no single individual can expect to provide a complete range of support that totally meets the needs of another person.

The steps involved in referring or transferring a person whose need you cannot meet to another, more appropriate source of trained assistance are as follows:

1. Have a working knowledge of the resources available in the community. Think in terms of interprofessional cooperation (psychiatrists, psychologists, social workers, counselors, and the like) and develop the ability to pinpoint who is outside your professional world that you need inside it in a particular situation.
2. Hint at the possibility of referral/transferal early after discovering the need for such action.
3. Present the need for referral/transferal to the person with care, in a sensitive, reassuring way:
   - Explain in detail what you perceive to be the person's need, based on what is emerging from the problem-clarification interview or the problem-solving process. Paraphrase and summarize the information the other has provided.
   - Explain why you cannot meet the need.

- Explain the appropriateness of a particular person or agency that might be helpful.

4. Remain silent and allow the person to express his or her feelings, accepting these as genuine and crystallizing any problems that might arise from the person's adopting the recommended alternative approach (for example, confidentiality, cost). Use the seven-step problem-solving process, as appropriate.

5. Be understanding but firm.

6. Reassure the person that you are not stepping out of his or her life and clarify specifically how your relationship will continue.

7. Expect him or her to feel rejected and respond to that rejection by helping the person get the hurtful feelings fully expressed and by letting the person know you have truly listened to those feelings.

8. To encourage initiative, follow up with the person, letting the other gauge the amount of follow-up required.

An Application of the Conflict
Resolution Model

L et us return to the Conflict Resolution Model and process described in the introduction and elaborated in the first book of this series. We can examine an actual conflict experienced by the authors of this book and see how the knowledge and skills incorporated in the model and process helped them work constructively and creatively with their situation.

Neil and Jack had coauthored a book on communication and conflict resolution skills. Because the subject area was new to the publisher, the editor asked Neil and Jack to design the cover. Each of them independently designed a cover before they met to discuss their two ideas. When they reviewed each other's design, they both noticed that each had themselves as the first author. After each had expressed his surprise and confusion, they met to discuss their differences around their seemingly incompatible positions:

Neil's Position: Neil's name first on the cover
Jack's Position: Jack's name first on the cover

Initially, Neil and Jack were aware they had a difference, but they weren't sure it was a conflict. As they began to discuss why they had each proposed what they did, they became aware that a conflict had emerged. They were mutually interdependent on each other, both were experiencing high emotion on the issue, and each of them was blaming the other for the problem and behaving in a way that was intended to prevail over the other through verbal persuasion. Even worse, while each of them attempted to justify the rightness of his position, he also began to denigrate the validity of the other's position.

Neil and Jack realized they were at a critical moment in the process. If they continued the behaviors they had easily fallen into, their justifications of their own contribution could easily escalate into attacks on the other and threats on what would happen if the conflict was not resolved amicably. Of course, the likely outcome of such behaviors would be that one party would win and one would lose (and be resentful) or that both parties would lose (and be resentful). Neil and Jack decided that those were unacceptable outcomes and decided to engage another strategy.

They considered three different strategies. (1) They could select a "fair" process and leave the outcome to chance by flipping a coin or letting an acceptable third party decide for them (namely, the editor). (2) They could enact a compromise solution—for instance, one author could have his name first on this book in exchange for a promise that the other author would be first if they were to write another book. They could then balance the risk and the gratification delay by giving the author who agreed to wait his turn a higher percentage of the royalties on the initial book. (3) They could attempt reaching a collaborative solution by preparing for and using an interest-based negotiation strategy. They decided that this was the wisest approach. They first managed the conflict by listening to and clearing out the negative emotion. They then identified each other's interests, created options, and selected the ones that satisfied the interests of both parties.

Neil and Jack realized it was important for each of them to prepare for this collaborative problem-solving strategy. They decided on their outcomes (to get their most important substantive needs satisfied while maintaining or enhancing their relationship) and selected a suitable, nondistracting neutral environment for their discussion. They reminded themselves to follow the conflict resolution process, attribute positive intention to the other party, stay resourceful, and maintain a positive attitude throughout the process. Most important to their success would be their ability to manage their emotions constructively, stay in rapport with each other, move away from positions to interests, and use their creativity and intelligence to identify and select among desirable and doable options.

The parties then entered into the conflict management process. Because building rapport, trust, and understanding was important in this early stage of their conflict process, they actively used reflective listening and pacing to enter into and understand the other's world as he was experiencing it. Critical to their success in this stage was their avoidance of reactive responses that would delegitimate the other's thoughts and feelings and make him more defensive. As they listened to each other with respect and integrity, and used chunking-up questions (Neil or Jack: "What would having your name first on the cover of the book do for you?"), they began to elicit and articulate each other's interests behind their positions.

These key interests emerged from their discussions:

Neil's Interests

- An outcome that was just and fair (relative to their contributions)
- A solution that would maximize book sales
- A solution that would aid his promotion and status at the university
- To maintain the relationship

Jack's Interests

- An outcome that was just and fair
- A solution that would maximize book sales
- Get books into print quickly
- To maintain the relationship

As Neil and Jack surveyed and discussed their interests, they uncovered useful information. Jack understood that Neil's promotion case at the university might be assisted by the listing of his name first on the book, and Jack, as an adjunct professor hired by Neil, could benefit by Neil's increased stature and autonomy. Jack also understood that Neil believed having his name first would sell more books, because he had higher name recognition among school personnel and they would likely be major purchasers of the book.

Neil then gathered important information from Jack about the interests that motivated Jack's position. Jack wanted a quick solution to the problem so the books could be printed quickly because he needed them for some upcoming workshops. Jack believed his name first would enhance sales because he had higher name recognition among business executives and ministry leaders, both of whom would likely be major purchasers of the book. In addition, both Jack and Neil agreed that maintaining their professional and personal relationship was important and that a just and fair outcome would reflect and recognize their different though equal contributions to the book.

Now that Neil and Jack each understood and accepted their collective interests as legitimate and well-intentioned, they could then move to a problem-solving process.

In Step 1, they formed a "How to . . . " statement based on their collective interests. The problem statement they agreed on was this: "How to deal constructively and creatively with the authorship dilemma in a way that would be just and fair to both authors, maximize sales from their respective constituents, enhance Neil's position at the university, get the book into print quickly, and maintain their relationship." They then moved to Step 2, brainstorming options.

In Step 2, they elicited ideas from each other and wrote them on paper to make them visible. Several solutions emerged. Some of these were the following:

- Rotate names on front and back cover.
- Use the words "coauthored by."
- Have an explanatory paragraph inside the book.
- Have the names on cover in circular fashion.
- Split royalties unevenly to compensate second author.
- Have two books with rotating authors.
- Have three books with Lawyer first on business and ministry editions and Katz first on the school edition.

In Step 3, they evaluated their options according to the criteria set forth in the "How to . . . " statement. The rotation of names was deemed to be confusing and might inhibit sales. The circular names and "coauthored by" solutions were just and fair but were seen as too unorthodox. The explanatory paragraph wouldn't eliminate the cover issue, and the royalty distribution was viewed as a compromise more than an integrated solution.

In Step 4, the "three-edition solution" was chosen as a first-choice solution because three distinct sectors (business, ministry, education) were identified as possible major purchasers of the book, thus maximizing sales. The solution would not delay publication significantly, it would enhance Neil's position at the university (colleagues would care most about the educational version), and it was deemed as just and fair (and practical) by the parties. Neil and Jack then developed an action plan to implement the solution.

In Step 5, they defined and specified next steps that were necessary to implement the solution, making sure they designated a "responsible person" and a specific timetable by which the action would be completed.

In Step 6, they set up a time in the future to check up on progress with the action plan and evaluated their process and the outcome.

In Step 7, they talked about the experience. They both felt excited and pleased about the respectful, affirming conflict resolution process they used to reach an integrated agreement that satisfied each of their interests without sacrificing or compromising anything of importance to either party. Both agreed that the process had led to creative solutions that were far superior in meeting their interests than any of the solutions they had individually come up with prior to their negotiation (their initial position).

Though Neil and Jack were feeling exuberant about their success in problem solving, they realized they needed the editor and publisher to agree to carry out their action plan. Their initial reaction to Neil and Jack's proposal was "No way!" "Three covers would cost more and eat into our profits." Neil and Jack were now feeling confident and competent with interest-based bargaining, so they chunked up the editor and publisher. They found out their primary interests were these:

1. Making a profit
2. Having high-quality books that would result in repeat customers
3. Keeping Neil and Jack as authors

Neil and Jack repeated the problem-solving process with the editor and publisher to come up with options that met the interests of all parties. They, and the publishers, listened respectively to each other's interests. They brainstormed options and eventually agreed on several that met their collective interests. To meet Neil and Jack's interests, the publisher agreed to keep the books priced at the original agreed-on price and to offer three editions. Neil and Jack, in turn, to meet the publisher's and editor's interests, agreed to rewrite the examples so that the language in each edition built rapport with the distinctive audiences (business, ministry, and education). This would insure greater quality and repeat customers. They also agreed to a "buy back clause" in which they would buy back, at publisher's cost, any unsold copies after 2 years. (This would ensure the publisher a profit, and Neil and Jack were confident in their sales projections because they would help market the books.)

After reviewing the agreement, the parties developed a plan for implementing the solution. In evaluating their process and agreement, each of the parties acknowledged that they were satisfied the solution met their interests. Furthermore, they were pleased to note that by working to satisfy the other party's interests, they had, in fact, come up with a higher quality solution to the problem than their initial position.

By reviewing this example from our life experience, we hope we have helped our readers understand and integrate the knowledge and skills we have presented in this book. By sharing our own efforts in using this approach, we also wanted to demonstrate our own strong belief in the viability and power of this model and process in helping us manage and resolve differences constructively and creatively. Although we are well aware that this model and process do not result in achieving win/win outcomes in every situation, we are convinced that the sophisticated use of the knowledge, skills, and attitudes presented in this book by our educational leaders will make a significant positive impact in our schools.

Annotated Bibliography and References

Carkhuff, R. R. (1977). *The skills of teaching interpersonal skills.* Amherst, MA: Human Resource Development Press.

An important work delineating strategies for teaching interpersonal skills to people in the helping professions.

Covey, S. R. (1990). *Principles-centered leadership.* New York: Simon & Schuster.

An innovative approach to leadership that balances security needs with guidance, wisdom, and power. Wide application of the leadership approach to work and family, professional and nonprofessional settings.

Drakeford, J. (1967). *The awesome power of the listening ear.* Waco, TX: Word.

An important work in the communication field articulating the powerful impact of highly refined listening skills.

Egan, G. (1976). *Interpersonal living: A skills/contact approach to human relations training in groups.* Monterey, CA: Brooks/Cole.

A useful book that presents some important distinctions between level and processes involved in developing empathy and enabling another to uncover meaning.

Fisher, R., & Ury, W. (1983). *Getting to yes: Negotiating agreement without giving in.* New York: Penguin.

A vastly popular book that has widely influenced the theory and practice of the negotiation field. A "hands-on, practical small book with numerous helpful examples."

Gordon, T. (1974). *Teacher effectiveness training.* New York: Peter H. Wyden.

A sequel to Gordon's influential and popular book Parent Effectiveness Training. *Informative chapters on "Conflict in the Classroom" and "The No-Lose Method of Resolving Conflicts."*

Katz, N. H., & Lawyer, J. W. (1983, Fall). Communication and conflict management skills: Strategies for individual and systems change. *National Forum, 63*(4).

The authors use an intervention in a large school system to describe their intervention decisions and philosophy, and their training approach in communication and conflict management skills.

Katz, N. H., & Lawyer, J. W. (1985). *Communication and conflict resolution skills.* Dubuque, IA: Kendall/Hunt.

A self-instructive, highly readable workbook with a variety of examples and exercises on listening, problem solving, assertion, and negotiation.

Laborde, Genie Z. (1987). *Influencing with integrity: Management skills for communication and negotiation.* Palo Alto, CA: Syntony.

A lively and provocative book that incorporates insights from neuro-linguistic programming to enhance the practice of advanced communication and negotiation. Very helpful chapter on making meetings work.

Margulis, J., & Richardson, J. (1981). *The magic of rapport: The business of negotiation.* New York: Avon.

An innovative work that applies the sophisticated communication strategies of neuro-linguistic programming to a negotiation context. Easy to read and use.

Nichols, R. G., & Stevens, L. A. (1957). *Are you listening?* New York: McGraw-Hill.

A scholarly book on the need for and importance of listening-skill training. Also includes 44 suggestions for listening exercises to use in the classroom.

Rogers, C. R. (1961). *On becoming a person.* Boston: Houghton-Mifflin. *A seminal work that, among other things, describes the powerful, theraputic value of attentive listening.*